One Dollar

MW01244230

One Store Too Far:

Saving Residential Neighborhoods

from

Dollar General Bulldozers

One Dollar General Too Far

One Store Too Far:

Saving Residential Neighborhoods

from

Dollar General Bulldozers

and

Why Some Towns Win

&

Others Lose

Ronald Fraser, Ph.D.

Foreword by Paul Wolf, Esq., President,

New York Coalition for Open Government, Inc.

Published by:

 The Cheshire & Company Viewpoints Publishing, Inc.

7744 Center Road, West Falls, NY 14170

Cheshire_Publishing@roadrunner.com

(716) 941-5986

www.smalltowncivics.com

*****

Cover Design by Carl Carbone

Printed in the United States of America

First Edition: October 2023

ISBN: 979-8-218-29494-6

The Peoples' Right to Know...

"The legislature hereby finds that a free society is maintained when government is responsive and responsible to the public...The more open a government is with its citizenry, the greater the understanding and participation of the public in government...The people's right to know the process of governmental decision-making and to review the documents and statistics leading to determinations is basic to our society...The legislature therefore declares that government is the public's business and that the public, individually and collectively and represented by a free press, should have access to the records of government..."

Source: New York State's Freedom of
Information Law

*****

"It is essential to the maintenance of a democratic society that the public business be performed in an open and public manner and that the citizens of this state be fully aware of and able to observe the performance of public officials and attend and listen to the deliberations and decisions that go into the making of public policy. The people must be able to remain informed if they are to retain control over those who are their public servants. It is the only climate under which the commonweal will prosper and enable the governmental process to operate for the benefit of those who created it."

New York State's Open Meetings Law

One Dollar General Too Far

CONTENTS

One Dollar General Too Far

FOREWORD

I first became aware of Ronald Fraser when I heard Ralph Nader interview him regarding his book, *American Democracy and You, Where Have All the Citizens Gone*? Nader described the book as "very engaging" and "a great discussion book."

We both share a passion for the citizen's role in democracy at the local level. His book highlight's the important role citizens can play in a town's decision to welcome or reject a Dollar General outlet.

I founded the New York Coalition for Open Government to promote government transparency and the right to have our voices heard at town hall, where elected and appointed representatives make decisions that greatly impact the town's quality of life.

Town meetings have long been an important part of our democratic history. The famous French historian Alexis de Tocqueville was fascinated by town meetings. In his 1835 report, *Democracy in America,* Tocqueville stated, "…local assemblies of citizens constitute the strength of free nations. Town-meetings are to liberty what primary schools are to science; they bring it within the people's reach, they teach men how to use and how to enjoy it. A nation may establish a free government, but without municipal institutions it cannot have the spirit of liberty."

For Tocqueville, participating in town meetings teach Americans how to become citizens in a democracy.

Once you exclude New York City, the average city, town and village in New York State has a population of 7,400. In fact, more than half of New York's 932 town governments are small and rural with a population under 3,000.

Towns, small and large, consist of neighborhoods with their own identities, characteristics and physical spaces. In the early 1900s, zoning laws came about as a way for communities to preserve and promote land use in a desirable and agreed upon way.

In New York State, town planning boards first came into existence in 1927, and today they play an important role in shaping community development by seeking to balance the interests of chain store developers and the public.

While zoning issues are hot topics, not enough attention has been given to how small town governments make planning and development decisions.

This book is unique. It takes a close look at how citizens and officials in three neighboring towns, operating under almost identical state and local laws, arrived at very different conclusions when addressing Dollar General's building applications. Here you will find valuable insights into how differently these town planning boards made their decisions.

Whether you are a citizen serving on a planning board, a citizen concerned about land use development in your community, or you are currently fighting for, or against, a development project in your community, this book will give you an inside view of democracy at the local level.

PAUL WOLF, Esq., President

New York Coalition for Open Government, Inc.

One Dollar General Too Far

PREFACE

This case study—prepared with the following audiences in mind—calls on readers to take a stand, to personally assess the actions of public officials.

Public Administrators. Even well-trained public administrators destined for careers in larger organizations, need a better understanding of the challenges facing untrained, rural, small town administrators.

Public administration skills are taught in dozens of New York State college and university degree programs. However, the textbooks used in these curriculums are mainly aimed at training public managers for careers in larger municipalities and in state and federal government agencies—not small town administrators.

This case study—an in-depth look at the decision-making processes in three smaller towns—will fill this curriculum gap.

Law Students. This case study will also provide valuable small town insights for law students taking municipal and zoning law courses.

Small Town Citizens & Officials. Beyond the classroom, this case study will help on-the-job government officials and concerned citizens take a hard look at how their towns are handling important public policy issues.

You Write the Conclusion

Chapters 1 through 9 provide a mainly descriptive account of the actions taken by officials in the Towns of Boston, Colden and Hamburg.

Along the way I have added my own critical comments, but have not attempted a final conclusion comparing the events in three towns.

Chapter 10 is where you, the reader can reflect upon the forgoing chapters and explain why officials in each town acted as they did.

ACKNOWLEDGMENTS

This report benefited mightily from:

The concerns expressed by citizen letter and email writers in the Towns of Boston, Colden and Hamburg, and;

The comments received on earlier drafts from these reviewers:

Peter Baker

Michelle Roberts

Mary Moglia-Cannon

Piers Wood

John Zack

And, four anonymous reviewers.

One Dollar General Too Far

INTRODUCTION

In the absence of a capable planning board,

a town's zoning ordinance is little

more than words on paper.

Studies of how well—or poorly—government officials conduct the public's business often start with a question.

Upon receipt of applications to locate similar Dollar General retail stores in three Western New York State towns, local officials were called upon to answer this question: Is the applicant's proposed location for building a Dollar General outlet consistent with the existing character of the neighboring community?

This study will search for the decision-making factors that guided town and planning board members as they reviewed their Dollar General site plans. To piece together the decision-making process used by officials in each town, we will review meeting minutes, looking for comparable insights into:

o The site plan review criteria deemed important by town and planning board members;

o How planning board members used their time; and,

o The nature of their interaction with both the Dollar General developer and the impacted citizens in each town.

Letters and emails sent from citizens to town officials, and citizen comments at public meetings expressing their concerns about the proposed Dollar General store, are also sources of information. We will identify:

o What most concerned the letter writers;

o How members of the appointed planning and elected town boards responded to their citizens' concerns.

THE STUDY'S METHODOLOGY

Chapter 1 sets-up the value-based zoning framework I have used to review planning board meeting minutes and citizen-written letters and emails in the three towns.

Chapters 2 and 3 apply this framework.

As reflected in planning board minutes, Chapters 4, 5 and 6 summarize the decision-making strategies used in each town. In the Towns of Boston and Hamburg meeting minutes provided a straight forward decision-making strategy. In the Town of Colden, however, further digging—beyond meeting minutes—was needed. Chapters 7, 8 and 9 take a closer look at how key decisions were made in the Town of Colden.

SOURCES of SITE PLAN REVIEW CRITERIA

Each town adopted a zoning ordinance setting out the site plan review criteria to be used by their planning board members (See Table 2). In addition, the State Environmental Quality Review Act's Full Environmental Assessment Form, Parts 1-3, sets out a second, independent, site plan review procedure for use by planning board and town board members.

Submitted site plans receive two reviews: One deals with on-site technical and engineering items; while a second review considers the proposed Dollar Generals' off-site impacts on the surrounding community.

For two reasons, this study will focus on the manner in which the three towns handled the off-site impacts of their proposed Dollar General applications. First, in each town the citizens' response to the proposed Dollar Generals overwhelmingly raised concerns about how the off-site impacts would likely negatively affect their quality of life.

Secondly, the denial of the Dollar General applications in the Towns of Boston and Hamburg were, in large part, due to the proposal's negative off-site impacts on the surrounding community.

THE CASE STUDY

Valuable insights can be gained by carefully following the manner in which a land use decision is made in a single town. And, comparing decisions across three towns will provide an even deeper understanding of how and why different planning board decisions were made.

The three Dollar General applications have a number of physical, legal and geographic characteristics in common, thereby strengthening their comparability. By limiting the influence of these factors we can more readily zero in on the specific actions of town and planning board members—the public officials in-charge of the site plan reviews—to explain the decision-making process in each town.

Population. Two of the towns are small, rural municipalities: Colden, with a 2020 population of 3,324 and Boston, with a 2020 population of 7,948. In addition, the Town of Hamburg, with a population of 60,085, will provide the opportunity to compare how a larger town handled a similar decision making event.

Geographic Proximity. The boundaries of the three towns connect one to the others. (See Map 1)

Building Size. In each case the same developer, The Broadway Group, proposed building a standard 9,000 square foot Dollar General retail store.

Parcel Size and Location. In each case the developer's proposed site plan covered one to two acres of land located in a predominantly residential neighborhood.

Parcel Zoning. In all three towns the site plan parcels were zoned commercial and in all three cases a retail store was a permitted use.

State Guidance. The same New York State Environmental Quality Review (SEQR) Act, including the law's site plan review criteria contained in Part 2 of the Full Environmental Assessment Form, applied equally to each town.

Town Zoning. In addition, in each town planning board members were required, by law, to apply similar site plan review criteria, (See Table 2), as prescribed in their town's adopted zoning ordinance. All three zoning ordinances called for the relationship between the proposed Dollar General stores and the surrounding residential neighborhood properties to be "harmonious."

Planning Board Recommendations. In the Towns of Colden and Boston town advisory planning board members sent their written— approval or denial— recommendations to the final decision makers, members of the town board. Comparison of these documents will provide additional insights into the manner in which each planning board performed their site plan review duties.

In the Town of Hamburg, the planning board members, designated the Lead Agency, were the final decision authority.

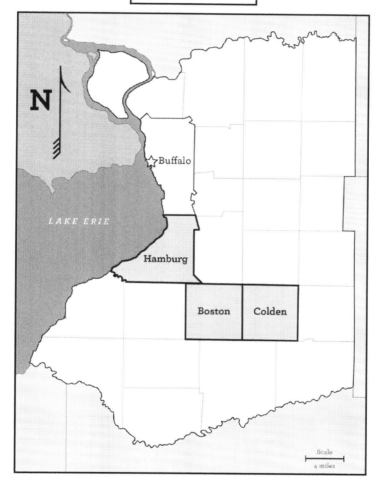

MAP 1
The Study Area

N

LAKE ERIE

Buffalo

Hamburg

Boston   Colden

Scale
4 miles

One Dollar General Too Far

CHAPTER 1. THE SITE PLAN REVIEW

Community values give a town's zoning ordinance its social context and its meaning.

Americans have long resisted granting too much power to government officials. To avoid European-style tyranny—placing excessive power in the hands of a ruler—American governments at all levels rely on adopted laws, including zoning laws, to establish the rightful authority to be exercised by their public officials.

In the absence of a binding zoning ordinance a town's land use development would become a chaotic free-for-all. If developers and town officials were free to do as they please, the wellbeing of town residents would be left to chance.

Importantly, in addition to establishing the rule of law, town zoning ordinances divide site development standards into two parts: The physical building standards and the non-physical, value-based, community development standards.

The Site Plan Itself. Planning board members must determine whether or not the physical site plan, the layout of proposed buildings and other infrastructure to be placed on the parcel, are compatible with the town's adopted zoning standards. This task is a well-structured application of technical and engineering standards contained in the town's zoning ordinance, and is often conducted by members of the planning board with help from outside, technical consultants.

The Site-plan's Community Impact. An equally important task calls on planning board members to consider how the activities to be conducted on the proposed site—in this case a retail store—will impact the quality-of-life of the people living in the surrounding, mainly residential, community. Does the proposed Dollar General store fit in with the existing character of the community? Does the proposed land use promote the non-physical, community development values imbedded in state and town site plan review laws?

Here engineers and outside technical experts are of little help. Unlike review of the site plan's physical components, this is a not a technical task. Instead, planning board members must gather qualitative, citizen-based input to decide, for example, whether the proposed Dollar General store, when in operation, will enhance or degrade the existing character of the adjacent community.

Towns do not adopt zoning ordinances for the benefit of land developers. Zoning laws are the visible expression of established community values held by the people who live there. Zoning laws supply developers with needed guidance to ensure submitted site plans will be consistent with these community values.

Definitions

Harmonious Relationship.

Harmony, a noun, is defined as, "the pleasing or congruent arrangement of parts...one lives in harmony with her neighbors," and,

Harmonious, an adjective, is defined as, "having the parts agreeably related; blended into a harmonious whole."

Consistency

Consistency, a noun, is defined as, "Agreement or harmony of parts or features to one another."

Inconsistent

Inconsistent, an adjective, is defined as, "Not compatible with another fact or claim; Contrasting incompatible elements."

Adjacent

Adjacent, an adjective, is defined as, "Not distant, being in close proximity"

Source: Merriam Webster's Collegiate Dictionary, Tenth Edition

*****

Using the above definitions, it is fair to say the term, "harmonious relationship," as used in the zoning ordinances in all three towns, and the term "consistency," as used in Question 18 of the SEQRA's Full Environmental Assessment Form, Part 2, calls on planning board members to determine whether or not the relationship that would be established between the proposed Dollar General store and the existing, surrounding land uses—mainly single-family dwellings—will form a pleasing, agreeable arrangement of land uses.

Community Character

"Community character is defined by all man-made and natural features of an area. It includes the visual character of a town...and it's visual landscape; but also includes the buildings and structures and their uses, the natural environment, activities, town services, and local policies that are in place. These combine to create a sense of place or character that defines the area.

"Changes to the type and intensity of land use, housing, public services, aesthetic quality, and to the balance between residential and commercial uses can all change community character.

"A comparison of current conditions to those that might exist after implementation of the project will determine if 'the action is inconsistent with the existing community character' or not."

Source: NY Department of Environmental Conservation, *Environmental Assessment Form Workbook, Question 18, Consistency with Community Character, Full EAF, Part 2*

Site Plan
NY Town Law 274-a, Site Plan Review

Definition of Site Plan. "A rendering, drawing, or sketch prepared to specifications and containing necessary elements, as set forth in the applicable zoning ordinance or local law, which shows the arrangement, layout and design of the proposed use of a single parcel of land as shown on said plan."

Approval of Site Plans. "The required site plan elements which are included in the zoning ordinance or local law may include, where appropriate, those related to parking, means of access, screening, signs, landscaping, architectural features, location and dimensions of buildings, adjacent land uses and physical features meant to protect adjacent land uses as well as any additional elements specified by the town board in such zoning ordinance or land use."

[Zoning ordinances in all three towns include an "additional element" in their site plan review criteria, specifically, consideration of whether a harmonious relationship will be established between the proposed Dollar General store and the existing adjacent land uses.]

Compliance with State Environmental Quality Review Act. "The authorized board shall comply with the provisions of the State Environmental Quality Review Act under Article Eight of the Environmental Conservation Law and its implementing regulations."

SOURCES OF ZONING VALUES

Site plan review criteria promote the community development values found in both the State Environmental Quality Review Act and in each town's locally adopted zoning ordinance.

Town-established Site Plan Review Criteria

Among the original reasons zoning ordinances were first enacted in the Towns of Boston, Colden and Hamburg is the protection of citizen-cherished community values. Table 1, compares the basic goals for the adoption of each town's zoning ordinance—goals that define the kind of home town its citizens want to live in.

Table 1. Why Zoning Ordinance Exist

Town of Colden	Town of Boston	Town of Hamburg
Zoning Ordinance, Section 108-3	**Zoning Ordinance, Section** 123-5	**Zoning Ordinance, Section** 208-5
Purposes and Scope, establishes the following specific purpose for the town's comprehensive zoning plan: "To preserve and promote the attractiveness of the Town of Colden." The comprehensive zoning plan was "formulated with reasonable consideration…as to the characteristics of each district and its particular uses,	Purposes and scope. "The comprehensive Zoning Law hereby established has been formulated with reasonable consideration, among other things, as to the character of each district and its particular uses and with a view toward conserving the value of buildings and	Purpose and scope. "The Comprehensive Zoning Plan hereby established has been formulated with reasonable consideration, among other things, as to the character of each district and its particular uses and with a view toward conserving the value of buildings and encouraging the most appropriate use of land in the most desirable

and with a view to conserving the value of buildings and encourage the most appropriate use of land in the most desirable manner."	encouraging the most appropriate use of land in the most desirable manner."	manner."

Zoning ordinances have been adopted to ensure their citizens will live in, and enjoy:

1. An attractive town;

2. A town where property value is protected; and,

3. A town where land is used in an appropriate and desirable way.

To further structure the conduct of site plan reviews, each town's local zoning ordinance has specifically identified (See Table 2) values-based criteria to be considered by planning board members during their site plan reviews.

Table 2. Site Plan Review Criteria

Town of Colden	Town of Boston	Town of Hamburg
Zoning Ordinance Section 108-116, Criteria for Planning Board Recommendations	Zoning Ordinance Section 123-167, Criteria for Review Recommend-ations	Zoning Ordinance Article XLIV. Site Plan Review Section 280-306. Criteria for Review Recommend-ations
A. The Planning Board shall review the site plan and supporting data before making its recommendations to the Town Board and take into consideration the following:	A. The Town Planning Board shall review the site plan and supporting data and take into consideration the following:	A. The Planning Board shall review the site plan and supporting data and take into consideration the following:

(1.) Harmonious relationship between the proposed uses and existing adjacent uses.	(1.) Harmonious relationship between proposed uses and design and existing adjacent uses and architectural features.	(1.) Harmonious relationship between proposed uses and existing adjacent uses.
(2.) Maximum safety of vehicular circulation between the site and street/road network.	(2.) Maximum safety of vehicular circulation between the site and street network.	(2.) Maximum safety of vehicular circulation between the site and street network.
(3.) Adequacy of interior traffic circulation, parking and loading facilities with particular	(3.) Adequacy of interior traffic circulation, parking and loading facilities,	(3.) Adequacy of interior traffic circulation and parking and loading facilities, with

attention to vehicular and pedestrian safety.	with particular attention to vehicular and pedestrian safety.	particular attention to vehicular and pedestrian safety.
(4.) Adequacy of landscaping and setbacks in regard to achieving maximum compatibility with and protection to adjacent property and land uses.	(4.) Adequacy of landscaping and setbacks in regard to achieving maximum compatibility with and protection to adjacent property and land uses.	(4.) Adequacy of landscaping and setbacks in regard to achieving maximum compatibility with and protection of adjacent property and land uses.

To comply with these zoning laws, proposed site plans submitted by developers must:

4. Promote vehicular and pedestrian safety;

5. Use landscaping and setbacks to achieve maximum compatibility with, and protection of, adjacent properties; and,

6. Establish an agreeable and pleasing relationship between the proposed land use and the surrounding neighborhood.

State-established Site Plan Review Criteria

Legally and administratively separate from the site plan review criteria established by town zoning laws, the State of New York has enacted a second, state-wide, site plan review process complete with both physical and cultural, values-based, review criteria known as the State Environmental Quality Review.

The state's site plan review criteria are found in Part 2 of its Full Environmental Assessment Form—consisting of eighteen site plan review questions, including a determination whether or not a proposed site plan will significantly impact surrounding properties with:

7. Emitted noise, odors and shining lights;

8. Increased auto and truck traffic;

9. An activity inconsistent with the existing character of the community; and,

10. Structures inconsistent with the predominant architectural scale and character of the adjacent land uses.

*****

Table 3, links each of the above ten community development values with a specific site plan review criteria promoting and protecting that community value.

Table 3. Community Values Shape Zoning Standards

Each of the Below Community Values…	…Form the Basis for Adopting One or More of these Zoning Standards
Source: Citizen-held Values	**Source: Town Zoning Ordinances** (See Table 1)
1. Pride in one's hometown	1. Preserve and promote the town's attractiveness
2. Financial security	2. Protect market value of private property
3. Take care of the land	3. Promote appropriate and desirable land use
	Source: NY State Environmental Quality Review Law
4. A clean, healthy neighborhood	4. Limit emissions of noise and odor and light shining onto surroundings properties
5. Personal safety	5. Avoid excessive auto and truck traffic

6. A stable living environment; fear of radical neighborhood change	6. Retain the existing character of the community
7. A stable living environment; fear of radical neighborhood change	7. Retain the predominant architectural scale and character of the community
	Source: Town Zoning Ordinances (See Table 2)
8. Personal safety	8. Promote vehicular and pedestrian safety
9. Personal property security	9. Achieve maximum compatibility with, and protection for, adjacent properties
10. A stable living environment; fear of radical neighborhood change	10. Ensure an agreeable, pleasing and harmonious relationship between proposed land uses and existing adjacent land uses

CONDUCTING THE SITE PLAN REVIEW

Two separate laws, two separate site plan reviews. While the town-enacted site plan review criteria, authorized by New York Town Law 274-a, and state-enacted site plan review criteria authorized by the State Environmental Quality Review Act, seem to overlap, they remain, at the town level, legally separate actions to be taken by local officials.

The eighteen site plan review questions promulgated by the State Environmental Quality Review Act are not a substitute for a town's own site plan review criteria established in its zoning ordinance. A developer's proposed site plan will, in practice, receive two separate reviews.

The state law, however, requires that town planners first complete reviewing the proposed site plan against the State Environmental Quality Review criteria; followed by a review of the developer's site plan against the town's own zoning established site plan review criteria.

One Dollar General Too Far

CHAPTER 2. THE VIEW FROM MAIN STREET

Table 3, lists ten community development values; the bedrock quality-of-life values held by the people living in the Towns of Colden, Boston and Hamburg.

Once aware of Dollar General's intention to locate a store in their town, what did citizens in Colden, Boston and Hamburg do? Well, they began to ask questions—questions concerning how a Dollar General store would impact their community, their property and what is near and dear to them—their quality-of-life values.

They also began writing letters and emails to town officials expressing their concerns. Less interested in the physical and engineering layout of the proposed Dollar General site plans, their letters and emails focused on how the proposed Dollar General store would likely harm what they valued most about their existing community.

Table 4 compares the Dollar General-related concerns citizens expressed in letters and emails sent to officials in the Towns of Colden, Boston and Hamburg. The table tallies the number of times the writers mentioned one or more of the ten community development values. Of the 63 letters and emails reviewed for this report, only one letter writer—in the Town of Hamburg— supported the proposed Dollar General store. All other writers voiced their opposition to the proposed Dollar General stores.

The same two concerns popped up again and again. Citizens in all three towns, by far, feared the negative impact the proposed Dollar General stores would have on the adjacent residential properties.

According to citizens in all three towns, the Dollar General stores would clash with the architectural scale and character of the adjacent properties, and fail to form a pleasing, agreeable relationship with the adjacent, established residential properties.

In addition, Hamburg citizens were also focused on safety issues. Many citizens in the Town of Colden, unlike citizens in Boston and Hamburg, criticized the manner in which their town officials were handling the Dollar General application.

Table 4.

Citizen Concerns Expressed in Letters and Emails

	Town of Colden	Town of Boston	Town of Hamburg
Number of Citizen Letters & Emails Sent to Town Officials	19	11	33
Community Zoning Values			
FROM TOWN ZONING LAWS (See Table 1)			
The proposed use does not preserve and promote the town's attractiveness.	6	0	1

The proposed use does not protect the market value of the surrounding properties.	2	0	1
The proposed use does not promote an appropriate and desirable use of land.	2	1	0
FROM TOWN ZONING LAWS (See Table 2)			
The proposed use does not promote vehicular and pedestrian safety.	0	0	10
Landscaping and setbacks do not achieve maximum compatibility with & protect adjacent use of property.	0	0	1

The proposed use does not create a harmonious relationship with existing, adjacent uses.	12	9	18
FROM STATE LAW			
The proposed use will emit unwanted noise, odor or light onto the surrounding properties.	1	1	7
The proposed use will significantly increase auto or truck traffic.	1	1	3
The proposed use does not keep with the existing character of the community.	12	9	15

	5	0	3
The proposed use is inconsistent with the predominant architectural scale and character of the surrounding land uses.			
OTHER CONCERNS			
	4	0	0
Planning board and town officials are ignoring the "harmonious relationship" site plan review criteria.			
	4	7	5
No need for another Dollar General store			
	3	0	0
The relationship between town officials and the applicant is too cozy.			

Town officials inaccurately claim they have no alternative but to approve the Dollar General store.	2	0	0
Town officials are not responsive to citizens' concerns.	3	0	0
Other locations are more appropriate for a Dollar General store	0	0	2

Map 2 shows the location of citizen letter and email writers living adjacent to the proposed Dollar General sites.

MAP 2
Residential Neighborhoods Surrounding
Proposed Dollar General Stores

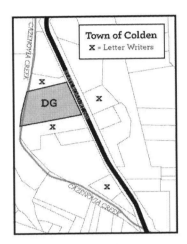

Town of Colden
x = Letter Writers

Town of Hamburg
x = Letter Writers

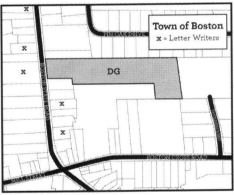

Town of Boston
x = Letter Writers

CHAPTER 3. THE VIEW FROM
TOWN HALL

The standards set out in zoning ordinances are not ends, but means to an end. The reason a town adopts a zoning ordinance—the sought after ends—are not-physical.

A zoning ordinance, in fact, is adopted for this singular purpose: To achieve the community development values held by the town's citizens; values that define the kind of town they want to live in.

While the first part of the site plan review includes attention to building setback distances, storm water flow volumes, etc., the second inquiry—the ten values-packed questions compiled in Table 3—measures the likely impact the proposed Dollar General store will have on the existing community, on the social and quality-of-life values prized by people who live in the surrounding, mainly residential, neighborhoods.

Only by carefully considering the ten value-laden site plan review items can planning board members determine if a developer's proposed use will, or will not, establish a harmonious relationship with surrounding land uses.

Table 5 compares the number of times—according to planning board meeting minutes—planning board members in each town considered whether or not the proposed Dollar General site plans were compatible with the ten value-based questions.

In the Towns of Boston and Hamburg planning board members, unlike planning board members in the Town of Colden, focused on how the proposed Dollar General stores would impact the surrounding community. The site plan review actions taken by planning board members in Boston and Hamburg tracked closely with the concerns expressed in letters and emails written by citizens in those towns—that the Dollar General stores would clash with the architectural scale and character of the surrounding community and fail to form a pleasing, agreeable relationship with the adjacent, residential properties.

Planning board members in the Towns of Boston and Hamburg, unlike planning board members in the Town of Colden, regularly invited and regularly discussed the concerns expressed by citizen in letters, emails and at public meetings.

Rather than spend time studying how the proposed Dollar General store would impact the surrounding community, planning board members in Colden focused their attention on the on-site, physical and engineering components of the applicant's site plan.

Table 5. Planning Boards Review Site Plans

	Town of Colden (Note 1)	Town of Boston (Note 2)	Town of Hamburg (Note 3)
Number of Planning Board Meetings	3	6	23
Community Zoning Values			
FROM TOWN ZONING LAWS (See Table 1)			

	0	0	0
Will the proposed use preserve and promote the town's attractiveness?	0	0	0
Will the proposed use protect the market value of the surrounding properties?	0	1	1
Will the proposed use promote an appropriate and desirable use of land?	0	1	1
FROM TOWN ZONING LAWS (See Table 2)			

Will the proposed use promote vehicular and pedestrian safety?	1	0	3
Will landscaping and setbacks achieve maximum compatibility with, and protection to, adjacent property and land uses?	1	1	2
Will a harmonious relationship exist between the proposed use and existing adjacent uses?	0	4	1

FROM STATE LAW			
Will the proposed use emit unwanted noise, odor or light onto the surrounding property?	2	0	6
Will the proposed use significantly increase auto or truck traffic?	2	0	3
Will the proposed use keep with the existing character of the community?	0	4	7

Is the proposed use consistent with the predominant architectural scale and character of the surrounding and uses?	0	4	**5**
OTHER REVIEW NOTES			
Number of times planning board members discussed neighbors' concerns	0	3	6
The Dollar General store has merit if proposed in a more harmonious location?	0	2	0

(1,) The Dollar General application arrived at the town on November 4, 2020. The Colden planning board held two site plan review meetings before voting to recommend that the Town Board approve the application. The first meeting was held on 2/16/21. At the second meeting, on 3/16/21, the planning board members voted to recommend that the Town Board approve the Dollar General application. Additional planning board meetings followed.

(2.) The Dollar General application arrived at the town on September 12, 2018. The Boston planning board held six site plan review meetings. The first meeting was held on 12/11/18. At the last meeting, on 12/9/19, the planning board members voted to recommend that the Town Board deny the Dollar General application.

(3.) The Dollar General application arrived at the town on July 17, 2020. The Hamburg planning board held twenty-three site plan review meetings. The first meeting was held on 9/19/20. At the last meeting, on 9/7/22, the planning board members voted to deny the Dollar General application.

CHAPTER 4. TOWN OF HAMBURG's DECISION-MAKING STRATEGY

Here, the actions taken by the Town of Hamburg's planning board members, as recorded in meeting minutes, will be used to piece together their site plan review strategy.

Having been designated the town's "lead agency," the Hamburg planning board's decision to approve or deny the proposed Dollar General would be final.

The Hamburg Planning Board met twice monthly to handle a significantly heavier workload than planning boards in the towns of Colden and Boston.

Planning Board Members: William Clark, Chair, Kaitlin McCormick and Doug Schawel, Vice Chairs, Jeb Bobseine, Margaux Valenti, Robert Mahoney, Dennis Chapman, Al Monaco and Megan Comerford

Town Land Use Planners: Sarah DesJardins and Andrew Reilly

Town Attorney: Jennifer Puglis

Town Engineer: Camie Jarrell

Applicant: The Broadway Group,
represented by Tara Mathias

*****

The Broadway Group's site plan application
to build a Dollar General store at 6505
Southwestern Blvd., was submitted to the town on
July 17, 2020.

August 19, 2020. Planning Board Meeting

Ms. Mathias, representing the applicant, said
she prefers access to the site from Southwestern
Blvd., a major arterial highway, but that the New
York Department of Transportation, for safety
reasons, prefers access from Heltz Road, a
residential street connecting with Southwestern
Blvd.

September 16, 2020. Planning Board Meeting

Chairman Clark, addressing Ms. Mathias: "The
proposed building does look very commercial, and
the area is residential/rural…the planning board
will be very interested in what the property owner
to the south thinks would be the most appropriate
buffer…the proposed driveway is directly across
from a residential home…what is proposed to
insure headlights do not shine into that property
owner's home?"

October 7, 2020. Planning Board Meeting

Ms. Mathias, says the building has been moved back 20 feet (from 11 feet) from the adjacent property to the south. NYDOT will not approve Southwestern Blvd. access. Shape of the building's roof and color options were discussed.

October 21, 2020. Planning Board Meeting

Ms. Comerford, a board member: "Proposed Dollar General building is not in keeping with the character of the community and looks like a straight box."

Mr. Reilly, a town planner, states that the planning board may have to issue a Positive Declaration under State Environmental Quality Review and require an Environmental Impact Statement asking for specific mitigations from the applicant.

Ms. Mathias stated that "she would be happy to have a conversation with the nearby neighbors."

November 4, 2020. Planning Board Meeting

Mr. Reilly notes that the Southern Overlay District requires that buildings maintain the rural character and appearance of the district.

November 18, 2020. Planning Board Meeting

Mr. Reilly: "Planning board should hold a public hearing and, based on Part 2 of the SEQR Environmental Assessment Form, to decide if the project will have a significant impact on the environment."

Chairman Clark schedules a public hearing to be held on December 16, 2020.

December 2, 2020. Planning Board Meeting

Ms. Mathias presents a revised site plan with access to the site from Heltz Road.

Mr. Reilly presents the completed SEQR, Full Environmental Assessment Form, Part 2, for planning board members to review and to decide, at a later date, if the Dollar General impacts on traffic, noise, odor and light and community character are significant.

Ms. Mathias says she feels the identified impacts can be remedied.

December 16, 2020. Planning Board Meeting

Public Hearing. Ms. Mathias says, "The applicant has worked hard to make the project fit in with the character of the community."

Neighboring residents' comments included:
Extreme opposition; poorly maintained Dollar
General in Blasdell; access on Heltz Road harms
quality of life for neighbors; store does not fit on
the lot; decrease in home values; social media
petition collected 1,000 signatures.

January 6, 2021. Planning Board Meeting

Public hearing continued.

Chairman Clark notes he has received many
emails from residents and said the planning board
will continue to accept correspondence on the
project until a few days before a decision is due.

Mr. Reilly: "SEQR is clear. If a project will
significantly impact the environment the planning
board issues a Positive Declaration....the planning
board cannot be sued over the issuance of a
Positive Declaration."

Chairman Clark: "The planning board members
really enjoy getting correspondence from the
public and are reading and listening to all input
received."

January 20, 2021. Planning Board Meeting

Mr. Rielly: "SEQR is clear. If a project may have a significant impact on the environment, the board is obligated to issue a Positive Declaration."

Board members reply:

Ms. McCormick: Supports Positive Declaration because of shining headlights, damage to community character and traffic.

Ms. Comerford: Supports Positive Declaration because of traffic and location of the access.

Mr. Chapman: Supports a Negative Declaration because no more information is needed.

Mr. Schawel: Supports a Negative Declaration because nothing is glaring enough to do otherwise.

Ms. Monaco: Supports Positive Declaration because of safety of pedestrians and traffic

Chairman Clark: Supports a Positive Declaration because of pedestrian traffic and access facing someone's home.

A Positive Declaration motion was made citing impact of noise and lights and impact on "the character and quality of the existing area and neighborhood," and pedestrian safety issues. The motion was approved 5 votes to 2.

February 10, 2021

Chairman Clark signed Part 3 of the State Environmental Quality Review form, "Evaluation of the Magnitude and Importance of Project Impacts," declaring that:

"This project may result in one or more significant adverse impacts on the environment, and an environmental impact statement must be prepared to further assess the impact(s) and possible mitigation and to explore alternatives to avoid or reduce these impacts. Accordingly, this positive declaration is issued."

Once a scoping document is received from the applicant, the Environmental Impact Statement process will begin.

May 5, 2021 Planning Board Meeting

Draft scoping document is received from the applicant

May 19, 2021. Planning Board Meeting

Draft scoping document is declared to meet SEQR requirements.

June 2, 2021. Planning Board Meeting

Planning board members hear area citizens expressing concern for the impact on the character of the community.

Mrs. Jablonski, a resident living on an adjacent parcel, states: "The impact of this project on the daily lives of the nearby residents regarding noise, dust and vibrations since the homes are so close to where the project would be located."

November 17, 202. Planning Board Meeting

Planning board member discuss the draft EIS.

December 1, 2021 Planning Board Meeting

Draft EIS discussed and a motion passed, 5 to 1, to declare the draft inadequate and identified 16 deficiencies, including that the applicant's draft EIS focuses too much on zoning issues and too little on community character issues.

January 19, 2022. Planning Board Meeting

Draft EIS found adequate by the planning board.

March 16, 2022. Planning Board Meeting

Mr. Reilly: "Planning board is responsible for the preparation of the final EIS…DEIS cannot be changed since it is the applicant's position."

June 15, 2022 Planning Board Meeting

Draft final EIS is discussed. Mr. Reilly: "The remaining issues of concern appear to be noise and light, community character, traffic, pedestrian traffic and others."

July 6, 2022. Planning Board Meeting

Discussion of the final EIS.

July 20, 2022. Planning Board Meeting

Final EIS reviewed. "Planning board members determined that additional measures are needed to protect the rural character of Heltz Road."

August 17, 2022. Planning Board Meeting

Mr. Reilly: "The issues, community character, the driveway location on Heltz Road and pedestrian safety…these issues led to the Planning Board indicating that the applicant has not mitigated them enough and they would have a significant impact." Further action was tabled.

September 7, 2022. Planning Board Meeting

The planning board members, acting as the SEQR Lead Agency, passed a motion, 5 to 1, issued a Negative Findings Statement denying the Dollar General application.

On September 21, 2022, Chairman Clark signed a State Environmental Quality Review Negative Findings Statement. While the applicant did adequately mitigate possible noise and light impacts, wastewater and storm water impacts, the applicant failed to mitigate to the maximum extent possible significant impacts on community character and traffic and pedestrian safety.

Mr. Clark stated that: "The project does not have any social, economic or other essential considerations that would outweigh the adverse environmental impacts that have been identified in the Final Environmental Impact Statement and articulated in these findings."

Meeting minutes show that, acting as the Lead Agency, the Town of Hamburg Planning Board's site plan review applied the criteria and procedures outlined in the State Environmental Quality Review Act, including the review

questions contained in Part 2 of the Full
Environmental Assessment Form.

Both the state review and the town's zoning
ordinance required the planning board members to
review the on-site physical and engineering
components of the proposed site plan itself for
consistency with state and local zoning standards.

In addition, the planning board members
were particularly interested in the off-site
relationship the proposed Dollar General store
would likely establish with the surrounding
properties and whether the site plan was consistent
with the existing character of the community.

Focus on Community Character. At its
second meeting, the Hamburg planning board
informed the applicant's representative that the
proposed building does not seem to fit well with
the existing, surrounding, mainly residential
properties. In subsequent meetings, planning
board members continued to look critically at the
potential impact of the proposed Dollar General
store on the surrounding neighborhood.

Throughout the review process the applicant
readily revised site plan items, such as the
building's design, to address concerns of both

planning board members and concerns solicited from, and expressed by, nearby residents.

Positive Declaration. But, at the seventh planning board meeting, members voted to issue a Positive Declaration, identifying traffic, noise, odor, light and community character as potentially significant environmental impacts requiring further evaluation and the preparation of a full environmental impact statement.

Step-by-step the planning board and applicant worked their way through the environmental impact statement procedures: The applicant's preparation of a draft environment impact statement; review of the draft by the planning board members; preparation of the final environmental impact statement by the planning board members.

But, in the end, Hamburg Planning Board members concluded that the applicant was unable to mitigate the proposed project's impacts on pedestrian and traffic safety and the proposed Dollar General's negative impacts on the existing community character. The planning board disapproved the project with the issuance of a Negative Finding Statement.

CHAPTER 5: TOWN OF BOSTON'S DECISION-MAKING STRATEGY

To piece together the decision-making strategy that guided the review of the proposed Dollar General site plan, this chapter will examine the actions taken by the Town of Boston's town and planning board members, as recorded in their meeting minutes.

The Boston planning board, an advisory body to the town board, made its recommendations to town board members who then made the final decision to deny the Dollar General proposal.

The Boston planning board met once a month.

Planning Board Members: Paul Ziarnowski, Chair., James Liegl, Vice Chair., Keith Pelkey, Elizabeth Schutt, David Stringfellow, David Bowen and Gary Stisser.

Tara Lowry is an alternate member of the planning board

Town Land Use Planner: Sarah DesJardins

Town Attorney: Sean Costello

Town Engineer: Michael Simon, LaBella Associates

Applicant: The Broadway Group, represented by Rebecca Hill & Melissa Ballard

*****

The Broadway Group's proposed Dollar General site plan for property at 9287 Boston State Road, was submitted to the town on September 12, 2018.

December 11, 2018. Planning Board Meeting

Chairman Ziarnowski informed Broadway's representative, Ms.Ballard: "This is a historical residential area. Even though you meet the code nuances, one of the things we have in general standards in our code is that 'proposed development shall be planned to harmonize with all existing and/or proposed development in the area surrounding the project site.' The concern is to put a box in the center of a residential area."

April 9, 2019. Planning Board Meeting

Chairman Ziarnowski announced this to be a public meeting "so that the Broadway Group can listen to what residents want to see there."

Earlier, an email from the Broadway Group advised the planning board members that a "neighboring meeting should not happen because it is likely people will be asking for things and upgrades that are not possible"

Ms. Hill presented a revised site plan.

Chairman Ziarnowski said the building is "still a square box."

Another board member said, it is a "very opposing, unfriendly looking building, it does not interrelate to any of the surrounding buildings."

July 9, 2019. Planning Board Meeting

Ms. Hill presented a new site plan and asked for a recommendation.

Planning board members asked about lighting and sight lines from neighbors.

Chairman Ziarnowski, still questions whether the site plan "conforms to the nature of that piece of property [and] made a motion to make a recommendation for the Town Board to deny the Broadway Group's application." The motion passed 4 to 1.

July 22, 2019. Planning Board Meeting

To follow up on the board's July 9, 2019 vote to deny the Broadway Group's latest site plan, Chairman Ziarnowski drafted a short, one paragraph letter to the Boston Town Board.

He wrote, "References in the code about maintaining integrity of neighborhoods and any new development or redevelopment to be compatible with the existing architectural flavor of the neighborhood were major factors in the decision. Without careful planning, residential properties in that area would have no incentive, with a lack of pride in their surroundings and unwillingness to invest. We could not condone doing [this] as a Planning Board thus rejected their proposal."

November 12, 2019. Planning Board Meeting

The planning board reviewed 45 issues the town's engineer and the Broadway Group's engineer had discussed, including trees, gooseneck lamps, setbacks, storm water management, the 30 vs 45 parking slots, two signs vs. one per the code, screening the HVAC, and many more.

A planning board member asked: "why the Planning Board was spending time on these details because he feels the project is not appropriate for the location."

Chairman Ziarnowski responded that the planning board is advisory and the town board does not have the time or expertise to go through the details, and added that he "feels the project has merit in a different location but still does not feel that the project is appropriate for the neighborhood."

He then made a motion to "recommend that the Town Board deny site plan approval because the proposed development is out of character with the neighborhood around the project site; a negative recommendation for the site plan." The motion carried 4 to 1.

December 9, 2019. **P**lanning Board Meeting

Chairman Ziarnowski drafts a two-page memo, dated December 9, 2019, to the Boston Town Board which read, in part:

"The Planning Board's recommendation to deny site plan approval is because while appropriately zoned, is of a scale and a use that is not harmonious with the neighborhood....Town Code 123-167(A)(1) requires that the Town Board and Planning Board must 'take into consideration' the 'Harmonious relationship between proposed uses and design and existing adjacent uses and architectural features.'...In this case, the parcel at issue might be appropriate for any number of commercial uses that are more harmonious.

"The proposed building remains a 'big box' sized and shaped general store that will conflict with the character of the surrounding neighborhood...there is no getting around the fact that the applicant is proposing a 'big box' retail store that is completely out of character for the design, mass and uses of the surrounding neighborhood. Therefore, the Planning Board recommends that the Town Board deny site plan's approval."

The Memo added, "A petition with over 1,100 signatures was gathered in opposition to this project. Many of the signers commented... that]...the scale of the proposed structure and use is not harmonious with the proposed location in an historic residential neighborhood. A copy of the petition is attached."

January 14, 2020 Planning Board Meeting

The planning board voted to approve of Chairman Ziarnowski's December 9, 2919 memorandum to the Town Board.

February 5, 2020. Town Board Meeting

The town board unanimously passed a two-page Resolution No. 2020-17:

"WHEREAS, Town Code 123-167(A)(1) requires that when considering an application for site plan approval, the Town Board and Planning Board must 'take into consideration' the 'Harmonious relationship between proposed uses and design and existing adjacent uses and architectural features,' and

"WHEREAS, Town Code 97-10(B) requires that 'Individual buildings shall be related to each other in design mass, material, place, placement and connection to provide a visually and physically integrated development, and

"WHEREAS, ...the proposed retail store...is out of character with the community in the proposed project location and of a design mass, scale and use that is not harmonious with the surrounding neighborhood...

"NOW THEREFORE BE IT RESOLVED that the Town Board hereby finds the site plan fails to conform to Town Code 97-10(B) and 123-167(A)(1); and,

"IT IS FURTHER RESOLVED that the Town Board of the Town of Boston hereby disapproves the final site plan submitted by The Broadway Group for development of a Dollar General retail store at 9287 Boston State Road.

"The foregoing Resolution was duly put to a vote on roll call which resulted as follows: Unanimous, five votes 'yes.'"

Meeting minutes provide an easily grasped record of the planning board's decision-making strategy—a simple, straight forward application of the town's adopted site plan review criteria found in the town's zoning ordinance, including:

Focus on Community Character. The planning board chairman, at the very first meeting with the applicant, established the town's central site plan review requirement: To be approved, applicant must demonstrate its proposed Dollar General site plan will form a harmonious relationship with the surrounding properties—a zoning ordinance requirement.

In meetings thereafter the applicant readily modified its site plan in response to concerns expressed by planning board members and nearby property owners, in particular concerns that that the proposed Dollar General store did not fit harmoniously adjacent properties and the exiting community character.

Input from Residents. Planning board members invited, and responded to, the expressed concerns of residents living near the proposed Dollar General site.

Planning Board says "No." At its third public meeting a planning board vote recommended that the town board reject the proposed Dollar General application.

The Boston town board formally denied the Dollar General application citing the site plan's failure to conform with the town's zoning ordinance, in particular, with Town Code 123-167 (A) (1), the harmonious relationship clause.

One Dollar General Too Far

Chapter 6: TOWN OF COLDEN's DECISION-MAKING STRATEGY

Here, the actions taken by the Town of Colden's town and planning board members, as recorded in meeting minutes, will be used to piece together their site plan review strategy.

The Colden town board and planning board met once a month.

<u>Town Board Members.</u> James DePasquale, Supervisor, Jesse Hrycik, Gerald Pietraszek, David Arcara and Patricia Zurbrick

<u>Planning Board Members.</u> Walt Kammer, Chair., Andrew Gow, Jackie May, Peter Newsom, George Reinhardt, Bobby Walker and Frank Hrycik

<u>Town Engineer</u>: Joe Wetzel

<u>Town Attorney</u>: Ron Bennet

<u>Applicant</u>: The Broadway Group, represented by Tara Mathias

****

The Broadway Group's November 4, 2020 application for a change of use for property at

8680 State Road, Colden, NY was submitted to the town on November 9, 2020. Part 1 of the State Environmental Quality Review Act's Full Environmental Assessment Form, was submitted on November 17, 2020.

December 3, 2020. Town Board Meeting

Town Supervisor, Mr. DePasquale: "The Change-of-Use process will go through the Planning Board, Environmental Board and if needed the Zoning Board of Appeals before coming to the Town Board for a decision.

"Social media has blown this meeting out of proportion, have faith in the Town Board working in the best interest for the Town. The Town Board must follow all laws and codes within the town...

"The Planning Board and Environmental Board have good people in place and will do a top-notch job reviewing this Change of Use. I urge anyone to write to the Town Board with their concerns. The Town Board will get through this in a professional and transparent way..."

Resolution #2020-11 was then adopted designating the town board as the lead agency to complete Parts 2 and 3 of the State Environmental Quality Review Act's Full Environmental

Assessment Form.

Approximately 33 residents attended the meeting via GoTo Meeting.

February 11, 2021. Town Board Meeting

Town Supervisor, Mr. DePasquale: "The Dollar General is not a done deal…the Environmental Board met to review the Long State Environmental Quality form. The Planning Board will meet to review the site plan and if needed the action will go before the Zoning Board of Appeals before the matter reaches the Town Board nothing is rubber stamped.
"There is a process to follow and if there are any concerns or problems the Town Board urges the public to talk with the Town Board members not on social media…"

February 16, 2021. Planning Board Meeting

Planning board members discussed with the applicant's representative, Ms. Mathias, site plan changes including engineering drawings, a traffic study, the Dollar General sign, building design and brick materials, softer lighting, storm water management, screening, the location of trees, how delivery trucks will navigate the lot, size of parking lot spaces…and more.

March 11, 2021. Town Board Meeting

Supervisor DePasquale: "If anyone has any concerns in town with any matters with the proposed Dollar General or any other matter, please do not hesitate to contact the Supervisor or any Town Board member."

March 16, 2021. Planning Board Meeting

Chairman Kammer turned the meeting over to Ms. Mathias, the applicant's representative, to give a revised slide presentation, including review of building designs, lighting options, a storm water plan and the need for only 30 parking spaces rather than the 52 parking spaces required by the town zoning code.

Handouts for the meeting, 37 of them, spanned November 2020 to March 2021, included: drawings, façade packages, the town engineer's report; the Code Enforcement Officer's Conformation of Compliance with Colden Chapter 108 Zoning, the Environmental Board's completed Part 2 of Full Environmental Assessment Form (dated February 3, 2021) and the Environmental Board's Advisory Report to the Town Board (dated February 16, 2021), and more.

Planning Board finding: Dollar Store "...is permitted per Section 108-44 (25)..."

Chairman Kammer, states that "…the variance about the total number of parking spaces proposed (30 vs. 52) is the only matter on this Change of Use which needs action by the Zoning Board of Appeals.

"All other known zoning and code issues have been resolved as related to the Change of Use…"

Chairman Kammer asked for a motion to approve the Change of Use application from the Broadway Group…motion made with the stipulation that the ZBA must resolve the number of parking spots and a vote was called. All in favor.

A Planning Board Recommendation to approve the proposed Dollar General project will be prepared and submitted to the Town Board for consideration.

April 8, 2021 Town Board Meeting

"Mr. DePasquale reported that the Town Board will host a Public Comment Meeting on April 22, 2021 on the proposed Dollar General at the Fire Hall. Pre-registration required." It was noted that this meeting was a "courtesy" gathering, not an official public hearing.

April 15, 2021. Zoning Board of Appeals Meeting

The Colden Zoning Board of Appeals grants Dollar General's request for 30 parking slots, not the 52 required by the town's existing zoning code.

April 22, 2021. Public Comment Sessions

Colden's Town Clerk, Christina Kerlin, prepared a written summary of the town citizens' remarks. Twenty-six citizens attended in person and 54 attended virtually.

Ms. Kerlin's summary listed 16 concerns and complaints voiced by the assembled citizens. The single most repeated complaint was the planning board members' failure to faithfully enforce the town's own zoning ordinance Code 108-116 A (1).

Ms. Kerlin wrote: "The audience stressed to the Town Board to consider Town Code 108-116, Criteria for Planning Board Recommendations: The Planning Board shall review the site plan and supporting data before making its recommendations to the Town Board and take into consideration the following: Section 108-116 A.(1), 'Harmonious relationship between the proposed use and existing adjacent uses.'"

Supervisor DePasquale stated that "the Town Board will take into consideration all of the comments and concerns while making a decision in this matter."

May 6, 2021. Planning Board Special Meeting

Chairman Kammer, reviewed, in full detail, the prior actions taken by, and documents prepared for, the planning board regarding the Broadway Group's intent to construct a Dollar General at their State Road property…

[he] reviewed the …the concerns from the Environmental Board, Planning Board, Zoning Board and the Town Board that were asked and answered or corrected by the Broadway Group…

[he] asked for feedback from Planning Board Members regarding the different color schemes submitted by the Broadway Group to be used for the exterior of the building."

Additional meeting items: (1.) Planning board members have put in 750-1,000 hours during the Dollar General site plan review; (2.) In response to a drawing presented by Ms. Mathias that was meant to show that the proposed Dollar General is a harmonious fit, Mr. Kammer remarked, "We dealt with that."

May 12, 2021, Planning Board Advisory Recommendation to Town Board

In a 13-page memo, Planning Board Chairman Kammer issued the planning board's Final Planning Board Advisory Recommendation to support its approval of the Dollar General application at 8680 State Road.

May 13, 2021. Town Board Meeting

In preparation for its June 3, 2021 meeting, Mr. DePasquale gives each town board member a packet including a copy of all prepared documents, and descriptions of actions taken to date, regarding the Dollar General proposal, including the planning board's final advisory recommendations report to the board (dated May 12, 2021) for their review, and copies of "Letters submitted from concerned citizens."

Mr. DePasquale states: "Town Board will have a review of the proposed project on June 3, 2021 [and] on June 10, 2021, the Town Board will have a final determination on the project."

June 3, 2021. Town Board Workshop

"The following points were made by Supervisor DePasquale:

"New York Town Law 261 empowers a Town to adopt zoning provisions. The Town exercised that power to adopt zoning provisions with the present Zoning Code in 1997.

"Article X of the Zoning Code as enacted provides the specific provisions regarding property within the Commercial District. The permitted uses are as a matter of right. Section 108-91(a)(25) lists "retail sales" as a permitted use.

[Editorial Correction: Section 108-44 A. (25), not Section 108-91, lists "retail sales" as a permitted use]

"An application for specific permitted use requires the Town Board to consider such use. Failure to accept a permitted use can result in a challenge based upon the action being arbitrary and capricious as a matter of law…

"In summary, the application for retail sales in conformity to the Comprehensive Plan, the Town Board must apply the Codes as enacted in the consideration of approval of a permitted use.

"The following Town Codes were read and stated.
        108-112. Site Plan required
        108-113. Procedure for review and approval

108-114. Authority to require additional supporting data
108-116. Criteria for Planning Board recommendations

"There was discussion from the Town Board and Planning Board Chairman Walt Kammer on mixed uses in districts and harmonious relationship between the proposed uses and existing adjacent uses.

"Public comment session was held which was not required but with the magnitude of this change of use one was held. Public received letters have been received and on file."

July 8, 2021. Town Board Workshop

Changes to the Change of Use Permit involving pollution discharge, storm water run-off, landscaping and the Dollar General sign were discussed and later acted upon during the regular meeting to follow.

July 8, 2021. Town Board Meeting

The Town Board unanimously approved an amended Change of Use Permit which read, in part, "This permit is contingent and subject to the following:

"1. <u>Code Requirements.</u> Full compliance with all sections of the Colden Code…

"2. <u>Site Plan.</u> …The Plan must comply with all Local and State regulations…

"5. <u>Planning Board Report.</u> …The Town Board has given careful and thorough consideration of the recommendations of the Planning Board in its consideration of the approval of the Change of Use Permit.

"15. <u>Storm Water Run-Off.</u> The applicant will be responsible for any Storm water run-off originating on its property which negatively impacts any surrounding properties."

*****

The Town Board then unanimously passed Resolution #2021-04 to approve the Change of Use Permit for the Broadway Group, which reads, in part:

"WHEREAS, …The Town Board acting as lead agency [reviewed Part 2 and] completed Part 3 [of the Full Environmental Assessment Form] and found that the project will result in no significant adverse impacts on the environment, therefore an Environmental Impact Statement is not required to be prepared and this Board has approved a Negative Declaration, and

"WHEREAS, the Town Planning Board has issued its report and recommendations at a meeting held on March 16, 2021 voting unanimously to approve the issuance of the Change of Use Permit…RESOLVED that the Town Board does approve the Change of Use permit…"

*****

Meeting minutes show, from the start, Planning board members in the Towns of Boston and Hamburg, took control of the decision-making process by applying, unambiguously, in full public view, Dollar General site plan review strategies that emphasized what is best for their community.

Unlike the straight-forward site plan review strategies applied in the Towns of Boston and Hamburg, town and planning board meeting minutes in the Town of Colden contain apparent decision gaps and fail to provide the reader with a clear understanding of the town's site plan review process.

For example, Town of Colden meeting minutes do not address the loud and clear concerns expressed by town citizens, suggesting the views of impacted citizens were not properly made a part of the town's site review process.

As a public record, Colden's meeting minutes seem to hide as much as they reveal. Instead of keeping the town's citizens informed, readers of the public meeting minutes are left to wonder what might be going on, unreported, in town hall.

The meeting minutes do, however, suggest the Town of Colden purposefully applied a site plan review that:

o Effectively removed town citizens from involvement in the site review process (See Chapter 7);

o Offered lip-service to the citizens' concerns expressed in letters, emails and at the pro-forma, public comment session;

o Was obsessed with Dollar General's on-site, physical and technical issues, while remaining willfully ignorant concerning the proposal's off-site impact on the surrounding properties (Town Code 108-116 A. (1)) and community character SEQR, FEAF, Question 18);

o Failed to address, early-on in the site plan review process, the Environmental Board's February 16, 2021 written comments to the FEAF, Part 2 questions—especially question 18,

"Consistency with Community Character"—informing Town and Planning Board members that the proposed Dollar General is not consistent with Colden's community character (See Chapter 9);

o Avoided dealing with a key site plan review criteria (Code Section 108-116 A. (1)) by attempting to redefined the meaning of the term, "harmonious" (See Chapter 8) and;

o Viewed the developer as a welcomed business partner rather than an applicant whose proposal must be carefully evaluated to determine whether or not it is in the best interest of the community.

CHAPTER 7.   BUREAUCRATIC RULES AT WORK

> "The public hearing provides a convenient and useful forum for citizens to play a significant role in the governmental decision-making process. As a general rule, local governments in New York State are required to hold public hearings whenever the action of the governing body can be expected to have significant impact on the citizenry."
>
> New York Department of State's *Local Government Handbook*

Meeting minutes show that in both the Towns of Boston and Hamburg citizens were, from the beginning, welcomed into the Dollar General decision-making process.

This, however, was not the case in the Town of Colden. From the very beginning, Colden officials relied on a bureaucratic, self-imposed rule to deny their citizens a meaningful role in the Dollar General decision-making process.

*****

On November 9, 2020, The Broadway Group submitted a—a Change of Use Permit Application—for property at 8680 State Road in the Town of Colden.

In response, a locally created, Change-of-Use form, set in motion a decision-making process bound by these two rules:

"1. F. A SEQR form [State Environmental Quality Review Act's Environmental Assessment Form] is not required for a commercial building under 4,000 sq. ft. Anything over 25 acres will require a full EAF-not usually a Type 1. A short SEQR [Environmental Assessment] form is usually all that is required."

"1.G. A Public Hearing is not required for a 'Change of Use.'"

*****

As written, Change of Use Rule 1.F anticipates that applications will be limited in both a building's square footage and acreage, and that a [less detailed] SEQRA Short Environmental Assessment Form "is usually all that is required."

On December 3, 2020, Colden's Resolution #2020-11 declared that "...the proposed [Dollar

General] project has been identified by the Town of Colden as a [State Environmental Quality Review Act] Type 1 action, based on the determination of significance [sic] impact which may be reasonably expected from the proposed action."

Since the proposed Dollar General building enclosed about 9,000 square feet, and due to the greater off-site environmental impacts associated with the proposed Dollar General, members of the town board, at their meeting on December 3, 2020 concluded that instead of using the "usual" short [less detailed] Environmental Assessment Form, in this case, a Full (SEQRA) Environmental Assessment Form would be required.

By requiring completion of a Full Environmental Assessment Form, Part 2, town officials committed themselves to deal with Question #18 on that form. Question 18 calls for the town to determine whether the proposed Dollar General is consistent with the existing architectural scale and the community character.

And, to do so, town and planning board members were bound to take into consideration the off-site impacts the proposed Dollar General store would have on the adjacent, mainly residential, properties.

What happened once the town board members determined that the Dollar General proposal was not an ordinary, low community-impact Change of Use application but, instead, a public decision with widespread community impacts?

Did the town board members seriously consider the advantages of waiving, in this high-profile case, their own, self-imposed, no-public hearings policy?

Rule 1 G. does not prohibit a public hearing. Instead, Rule 1.G—as well as common sense—allows town board members to hold public hearings whenever they see a need for public input into their decision-making process.

Did they consider how bringing citizens—especially those citizens directly impacted by the proposal— into the Dollar General site plan review process would better inform their decision to approve or deny the application?

Or, did they unthinkingly, bureaucratically, cling to Rule 1. G?

Answers to these key questions are not found in the public record. But, by choosing to enforce the Change of Use, "no public hearing" rule, the town board members created an enduring tug-of–war between town hall and the town's citizens.

In addition, by using Change of Use Rule 1.G as an excuse to block citizen participation, members of the town and planning boards were free to take less seriously state and town site plan review procedures.

To allow citizen participation would cast a bright light on the Dollar General's off-site, neighborhood impacts. By keeping citizens at bay, town and planning board members were free to focus their attention on on-site engineering and technical details and ignore significant off-site impacts of the proposed Dollar General on the citizens living in the nearby neighborhood and on the community.

The record suggests that town officials, from the start, sought to quickly approve the Dollar General proposal. To involve citizens would only complicate their decision-making process. By not waiving Rule 1, G, the town board members set in motion events that effectively discouraged any meaningful public participation in the Dollar General site plan review process.

Since, historically, Change of Use Rule 1.F anticipated changes with low-level, off-site environmental impacts, and "a short SEQR [Environmental Assessment] form is usually all that is required," it may have made sense in past years for the town to establish a rule for opting-out of public hearings.

But once town board members concluded on December 3, 2020, that the proposed Dollar General was a Type-1 action, including the possibility for high environmental impacts on the surrounding properties and community character, town planners should have recognized the need to bring Colden citizens into the Dollar General decision-making process.

By clinging to Rule 1.G, Town of Colden officials adopted a Dollar General decision-making process that shut down any meaningful communications between the town's citizens and their elected and appointed officials. From this early point going forward, Colden citizens—unlike citizens in the Towns of Boston and Hamburg—

were denied their rightful role as participants, as stakeholders, in a major land use decision certain to impact their established small town, rural life style.

Colden citizens were denied a chance to attend, observe, and listen to their town officials deliberate—in open Planning Board meetings— their concerns of the Dollar General's off-site impacts. If, according to meeting minutes these deliberations and decisions did not take place in open Town and Planning Board meetings, they were either made out of public view, or not at all.

Members of the Colden Town Board, at their first two meetings in December of 2020 and February 2021, encouraged citizens to send their Dollar General concerns to them and not to protest on social media. This invitation to participate in the Dollar General review appeared, at first, to be an honest invitation, that the door was open for citizens to take part in the decision making process.

Instead, with the passage of time, it looked more like an attempt by the town board to disarm and marginalize—not to deal with—the legitimate concerns of the town's citizens. As a result, many citizens suspected their elected officials, from the start, treated the Dollar General proposal as a done deal.

CHAPTER 8. HOW RULES CREATE A CATCH-22

> "I don't know what you mean by 'glory,'" Alice said.
>
> Humpty Dumpty smiled contemptuously. "Of course you don't—till I tell you...
>
> "When I use a word," Humpty Dumpty said, in a rather scornful tone, "it means just what I choose it to mean—neither more nor less."
>
> *Through the Looking-Glass*, by Lewis Carroll, 1872

In very clear English, almost identical zoning laws adopted in the Towns of Colden, Boston and Hamburg (See Table 2), established criteria to be used by town officials deciding whether site plans submitted by the Dollar General developer, The Broadway Group, should be approved or rejected.

In each town, these criteria require planning board members to consider whether or not the relationship between the proposed Dollar General store and the existing adjacent land uses would be "harmonious."

To establish this relationship, however, would require bringing the concerns of citizens, especially those living nearby the proposed Dollar General site, into the site review process.

In the Towns of Boston and Hamburg meeting minutes show that planning board members did, in fact, follow the law and carefully considered the relationship to be established between the proposed Dollar General stores and the surrounding land uses.

Meeting minutes for the Town of Colden, however, tell a different story. Planning and Town Board members in Colden, during their reviews of the Dollar General site plan, avoided publicly dealing with the town's Section 108-116 A. (1), "harmonious relationship" review requirement.

Caught in a bureaucratic Catch-22, Colden officials found themselves trapped in a tug-of-war between two self-imposed rules.

The town's Change of Use Permit rule (See Chapter 7), blocked citizen participation in the town's site plan review process.

However, to satisfactorily comply with another rule—the town's zoning ordinance law, Section 108-116 A. (1), the harmonious relationship clause—town officials are obliged to consider off-site impacts of the proposed Dollar General store on the surrounding community. This, in turn, would require bringing the concerns of citizens, especially those living in the nearby neighborhood, into their Dollar General review process.

Colden's Catch-22 dilemma: How to satisfy the harmonious relationship rule while, at the same time, banning the participation of citizens directly impacted by the proposed Dollar General store?

Using available public records, here is how Town of Colden officials plotted their way out of the Catch-22 dilemma:

o Keep harmonious relationship discussion items off of public meeting agendas;

o Don't publicly respond to the Dollar General concerns expressed in citizen-written letters and emails;

o Rapidly gain the planning board's approval and kick the harmonious relationship can down the road;

o Hold pro-forma, non-official, public venting sessions <u>after</u> the planning board members had officially recommended approval of the Dollar General proposal;

o Maneuver around the Section 108-116 A. (1) rule by redefining the meaning of "harmonious relationship."

*****

The Broadway Group's November 4, 2020 application for a change of use for the property located at 8680 State Road was submitted to the town on November 9, 2020.

At early Dollar General meetings in the Towns of Boston and Hamburg, town officials put The Broadway Group's representatives on notice that there were problems with the proposed location of their stores; that there appears to be a conflict between the location of their proposed Dollar Generals and the surrounding community and nearby residential properties.

In the Town of Colden, word spread quickly that a Dollar General was in the works. Citizens, alarmed that the proposed Dollar General did not fit in the surrounding, mainly residential neighborhood, turned to social media to broadcast their protests.

December 3, 2020 Town Board Meeting.

At its first official meeting since the arrival of the Dollar General application, the Colden town supervisor, Mr. DePasquale, did not address the particular concerns being widely expressed by the town's citizens. Nor did he build trust among the citizens that the town would, in fact, take a hard look at the relationship between the proposed Dollar General store and the surrounding community.

Instead, he tried to downplay the importance of the citizens' concerns already being expressed on social media, saying: "Social media has blown this meeting out of proportion…" He urged the citizens of Colden to "…have faith in the Town Board working in the best interest for the Town…"

And he urged "…anyone to write to the Town Board with their concerns."

That they did. Twelve of the 19 letters and emails town officials received from citizens (See Appendix A) called on the town and planning board members to follow the law, to comply with Section 108-116 A.(1) and to conclude the proposed Dollar General store was not a "harmonious" fit in the existing neighborhood.

February 11, 2021, Town Board Meeting.

At gatherings around town and on social media, Colden citizens continued their protests. Rumors spread that the town's officials were prepared to approve the Dollar General application.

At this, the second official opportunity for town officials to respond directly to the main concerns of their citizens—that town officials were not taking the citizens' loudly and clearly expressed concerns seriously—the meeting failed to reassure anxious citizens.

Instead, Mr. DePasquale, dismissing the concerns being sent from citizens to town hall during the past two months, said, "…if there are any concerns or problems the Town Board urges the public to talk with the Town Board members not on social media." If?

Rather than reassure the citizens by directly responding to the rumors that the town was prepared to approve the Dollar General application, Mr. DePasquale made this remarkable statement: "The Dollar General is not a done deal…nothing is rubber stamped…"

Many citizens in Colden took that unsolicited denial as an affirmation that, indeed, the rumors were credible, that town hall had stacked the deck against the citizens.

February 16, 2021, Planning Board Meeting.

This, the first open meeting of the planning board was a critical opportunity for the town to reassure its citizens that members of the planning board were, in fact, addressing their Dollar General concerns.

Instead, missing from the meeting agenda was any reference to zoning ordinance Section 108-116 A. (1)—consideration of the nature of the relationship between the Dollar General store and the off-site, surrounding neighborhood—a required site plan review criteria.

Planning board members focused on engineering drawings, a traffic study, the Dollar

General sign, building designs and brick materials, softer lighting and storm water management.

March 11, 2021, Town Board Meeting.

Once again, the well-publicized citizen concerns about off-site, neighborhood impacts of the proposed Dollar General store, were not addressed. Supervisor DePasquale's message: "If anyone has any concerns in town with any matters with the proposed Dollar General or any other matter, please do not hesitate to contact the Supervisor or any Town Board member."

"If?" Was the supervisor serious? How could he not have been aware of the citizen concerns awash in the town for months?

March 16, 2021, Planning Board Meeting.

This, the second open Dollar General Planning Board Meeting, was a prime opportunity for the planning board members to reassure citizens that they were being heard in town hall.

But, again, Zoning Section 108-116 A. (1)— the nature of the relationship between the Dollar General store and the surrounding neighborhood— was not on the agenda.

Nor was the Environmental Board's Advisory Report to the town board, dated February 16, 2021, on the agenda. The Environmental Board's response to the Full Environmental Assessment Form's Part 2, Question 18, raised this red flag for review by the planning board members:

"The proposed action [the proposed Dollar General store] is inconsistent with the existing community character…the proposed action is inconsistent with the predominant architectural scale and character" of the community.

No response from the planning board members.

Avoiding any reference to still unfulfilled, mandatory site plan review requirements, Chairman Kammer states that, with the exception of the number of parking spaces yet to be approved by the Zoning Board of Appeals, "All other known zoning and code issues have been resolved as related to the Change of Use…"

A motion was then made, and unanimously approved by the planning board members, to send to the town board the planning board's recommendation to approve the proposed Dollar General application.

The planning board members kicked the harmonious relationship can further down the road.

April 22, 2021, Public Comment Sessions.

After announcing that the town board members do not need public input for their Dollar General review, the town offered citizens a pro-forma, one-way communication forum to publicly unload their displeasure with how the town was handling of the Dollar General review.

This was not an official public hearing where citizens are empowered to officially confront their elected representatives. This was an off-the-record event. After all, the Change of Use rule allows for no citizen input.

That this gathering took place one month after the planning board members had voted to approve the Dollar General application—reinforcing the appearance of a done deal—further underscored the town administration's determination to keep citizen participation out of their decision-making process.

Twenty-six citizens attended in person and 54 attended virtually.

The single most repeated complaint: The planning board's failure to follow the town's own law, and that Planning Board members voted to approve the Dollar General application without addressing the harmonious relationship clause in the town's zoning ordinance, Section 108-116 A (1).

Here is how Colden's Town Clerk, Christine Kerlin, summarized the citizens' remarks:

"The audience stressed to the Town Board to consider Town Code 108-116, Criteria for Planning Board Recommendations: The Planning Board shall review the site plan and supporting data before making its recommendations to the Town Board and take into consideration the following: Section 108-116 A.(1), 'Harmonious relationship between the proposed use and existing adjacent uses.'"

The event ended without a single response to the angry citizens from town and planning board members in attendance. Supervisor DePasquale later said: "A public comment session was held which was not required but with the magnitude of this change of use one was held.

May 6, 2021, Planning Board Special Meeting.

Having already voted to recommend approval of the proposed Dollar General to the town board, Chairman Kammer, asked for feedback from planning board members regarding the different color schemes that were submitted by the Broadway Group for the exterior of the building.

In response to a drawing presented by Ms. Mathias, the Broadway representative, a drawing she claimed showed that the proposed Dollar General is a harmonious fit in the surrounding properties, Mr. Kammer remarked, "We dealt with that."

No details were given as to when, where, or in what manner the planning board members had dealt with the "harmonious fit" question.

May 12, 2021. The planning board issued its 13-page, Final Planning Board Advisory Recommendation to Town Board recommending approval of the Dollar General application. By not directly addressing Section 108-116 A. (1) in its report, the planning board members once again kicked the harmonious relationship can down the road.

The planning board members did, however, reference in its Final Planning Board Advisory Recommendation to Town Board, a document prepared by The Broadway Group, the applicant, declaring their proposed Dollar General to be a harmonious fit. (See Chapter 9)

June 3, 2021, Town Board Workshop.

It was clear from the beginning, the harmonious relationship can could be kicked just so far down the road. Sooner or later, the day would come when members of the town and planning boards would need to devise an administrative maneuver to render Code Section 108-116 A. (1) irrelevant.

That day arrived on June 3, 2021. Among the other items contained in the minutes for this meeting (See Chapter 6), is this sentence that hid more than it revealed:

"There was discussion from the Town Board and Planning Board Chairman Walt Kammer on mixed uses in districts and harmonious relationship between the proposed uses and existing adjacent uses."

Finally, after so many public Town and Planning Board meetings that successfully avoided dealing with the impacts of the proposed Dollar General store on the surrounding community, it appeared the time had arrived for town officials to take seriously Code Section 108-116 A. (1) and discuss the "harmonious relationship between the proposed uses and existing adjacent uses."

I attended, and took notes during the June 3, 2021 workshop proceedings. To verify my recollection of the harmonious relationship discussion that took place between the town supervisor and the planning board chairman, I asked to review the town's audio recording of the meeting.

On November 3, 2022, the town clerk confirmed that the audio recording of the June 3, 2021 town board workshop no longer existed. After approval of the written minutes of that meeting she, as was her custom, erased the audio recording.

Therefore, the following account is based on notes taken by me and others at the time of the discussion. That discussion—an attempt to redefine the meaning of "harmonious relationship"—proceeded as follows:

Code Section 108-44, Permitted Uses and Structures, is a single list of 42 permitted uses. Permitted use Number 1 is a single-family dwelling, and permitted use Number 25 is a retail sales structure. Because single-family dwellings and retail sales structures are found in the same Section 108-44 list, they automatically, ipso facto, form a harmonious relationship.

Both Mr. Kammer, the planning board chairman, and Mr. DePasquale, the town board supervisor, agreed to this illogical reasoning.

In their attempt to satisfy the requirements of Code Section 108-116 A. (1) with a fallacious definition of "harmonious relationship," Misters Kammer and DePasquale commit a logical fallacy and reach this erroneous conclusion: The location of the proposed Dollar General store adjacent to single family dwellings along Route 240, north of the Rt. 240/Boston-Colden/Heath Roads intersection in the Colden Hamlet, enjoys, per Section 108-44, a harmonious relationship.

Logically, the hodge-podge collection of permitted uses and structures listed in Code Section 108-44—commercial car washes, bowling allies, single family dwellings, retail stores, etc.— share one, and only one, property in common: that is, they are all permitted uses and structures.

There is no logical, epistemological or legal basis to claim this collection of permitted uses and structures listed in Code Section 108-44 are somehow, automatically, harmoniously related one to the other simply because they appear in a single list.

Merriam Webster's Collegiate Dictionary, Tenth Edition:

"Harmony," a noun, is defined as the pleasing or congruent arrangement of parts…one lives in harmony with her neighbors, and,

"Harmonious," an adjective, is defined as having the parts agreeably related; blended into a harmonious whole.

Nowhere in these dictionary definitions is there reference to a "list." What these definition do establish, however, is that an agreeable relationship will exist between any two uses listed in Code Section 108-44 if, and only if, upon close examination the two uses form a pleasing, agreeable, harmonious whole.

One Dollar General Too Far

CHAPTER 9

NEW YORK STATE's ENVIRONAMTAL QUALITY REVIEW

To better understand how the statewide and local site plan reviews must work together, let's start with a few passages from the State Environmental Quality Review Act (SEQRA). Here is why New York State Legislators said they passed this law.

"The basic purpose of SEQR is to incorporate the considerations of environmental factors into the existing planning, review and decision-making processes of state, regional and local government agencies at the earliest possible time...It is not the intention of SEQR that environmental factors be the sole consideration in decision-making....[and, as a general rule]...The lead agency will make every reasonable effort to involve project sponsors, other agencies and the public in the SEQR process."

Three important points here:

Point One. The state law does not supersede locally-enacted site plan review criteria adopted in a town's zoning ordinance. Instead, the state's site plan review criteria contained in Parts 1-3 of its

Full Environmental Assessment Form are to be applied alongside, in addition to, the town's existing review criteria.

Point Two. To effectively guide the town's site plan review actions, the state's Full Environmental Assessment Form, especially review criteria in Parts 1 and 2, are to be addressed by town planners at the earliest possible time.

According to guidance in the Full Environmental Assessment Form: "When Part 2 is completed, the lead agency will have identified the relevant environmental areas that may be impacted by the proposed activity."

An early completion of the 18 site plan review questions contained in Part 2 allows time for town planners to conduct a thorough analysis of the impacted areas and to provide timely and trustworthy advice to the town board members well in advance of their completion of the Full Environmental Assessment Form, Part 3.

Point Three. Involvement of the town's citizens in the decision-making process, especially those citizens directly impacted by the proposed Dollar General store is a key part of the site plan review and decision-making process.

For each of the 18 site plan review questions in Part 2 where the impact has been "...identified as potentially moderate to large or where there is a need to explain why a particular element of the proposed action will not, or may, result in a significant adverse environmental impact," the town's Lead Agency, in Part 3, is required to provide a written explanation of the steps taken to mitigate these potential impacts, or to indicate that the potential impacts have not been mitigated.

Table 6 compares how Lead Agencies in the Towns of Colden and Hamburg handled the state's Full Environmental Assessment Form, Part 2, Question 18.

Table 6. Full Environmental Assessment Form, Part 3

Town of Colden Environmental Board's Written Report to the Town Board in Response to SEQRA, Environmental Assessment Form, Part 2, Question 18, Consistency with Community Character February 16, 2021 ***** "The proposed project is	Town of Colden Town Board's (Lead agency) Part 3 Response to SEQRA, Environmental Assessment Form, Part 2, Question 18, Consistency with Community Character June 10, 2021 ***** In response to the Environmental Board's February 16, 2021 findings	Town of Hamburg Planning Board's Written Response to the SEQRA, Environmental Assessment Form, Part 2, Question 18, Consistency with Community Character February 10, 2021 ***** "The proposed project is in sharp contrast to the

inconsistent with the existing community character…and with the predominant architectural scale and character…

"A survey of Colden town residents taken before the current Master Plan was created found that residents sought to: Preserve the town's picturesque and small town character…

"Preserve the town's rural,

that the proposed Dollar General is "inconsistent with predominant architectural scale and character," the Town Board declared on June 10, 2021:

"The Applicant has worked with the Town to make reasonable changes to enhancing the façade of the building. A survey of other businesses in the immediate vicinity of the proposed Site

surrounding land uses…

"The proposed building is not consistent with the architectural scale of the area…

"The proposed project will alter the essential character of the area."

*****

The Planning Board then required a full Environmental Impact Statement be prepared. The EIS, however,

agricultural
heritage and
avoid
conflicting land
uses…
    "The
construction of
a 9,000 plus
square foot
concrete block
building very
close to the
center of town
strongly
conflicts with
these stated
desires of town
residents…
    "The Master
Plan also seeks
to 'promote
local business.'
The Dollar
General
Company is not
a local
business. It is a

(as compiled in
the Planning
Boards Final
Report, 4-29-
21) shows that
there are other
businesses of
similar scale
and look to the
proposed
store."
    *****
    The Town
Board then
approved the
proposed
Dollar General
store with this
declaration:
"This project
will result in
no significant
adverse
impacts on the
environment,
and, therefore
an

failed to
mitigate the
project's
adverse
impacts, and
the Dollar
General
application was
denied.

national chain. In other rural communities where the chain has built stores, local grocery business owners are often driven out of business… "Our current local businesses provide healthier fresh foods that contribute not only to a community's overall health but also to its resiliency."	environmental impact statement need not be prepared."	

Let's take a closer look at Colden Town Board's response to the Full Environmental Assessment Form, Question 18.

How did members of the Town Board determine, in June 2021, that the proposed Dollar General store was, indeed, consistent with the character of the adjacent neighborhood when— four months earlier—the town's Environmental Board, in response to the same Question 18, advised the Town Board members: "The proposed action is inconsistent with the predominant architectural scale and character."

Concluding that the Full Environmental Assessment Form, Part 2, including the Question #18 red flag raised above by the Environmental Board, is a matter for consideration by the lead agency, the Town Board, there is no public record that the Planning Board ever rendered an independent analysis to determine whether or not the proposed Dollar General, contrary to the Environmental Board's Question #18 response, is inconsistent with the existing architectural scale and community character.

Consequently, the Town Board members were on their own regarding how to respond to the Environmental Board's conclusion that the proposed Dollar General was inconsistent with the existing architectural scale and community character.

How then did members of the Town Board mitigate the Environmental Board's claim that the proposed Dollar General was inconsistent with the predominant architectural scale and character of the surrounding properties?

In his Part 3 response, the Colden town supervisor declared: "A survey of other businesses in the immediate vicinity of the proposed Site (as compiled in the Planning Boards Final Report, 4-29-21) shows that there are other businesses of similar scale and look to the proposed store."

What evidence did members of the Town Board consider in making this key decision? And what was the source of that evidence; who prepared the referenced survey? How did the survey's author define "immediate vicinity"?

Reference to "4-29-21" in Mr. DePasquale's Part 3 declaration is misleading. It refers to a self-serving report prepared by, and received from, the applicant, The Broadway Group, on 4-29-21—at the request of the town's planning board chairman.

The clear intent of The Broadway Group's report was to discredit the many citizens who, during the April 22, 2021 public comments sessions, accused the town of not enforcing

Section 108-116 A. (1), and who repeatedly declaring the proposed Dollar General was both a non-harmonious use and inconsistent with the town's community character.

The Broadway Group's report was an attempt to persuade the planning board members that the proposed Dollar General store forms a harmonious relationship with the adjacent residential properties.

Dozens of citizens told the town and planning board members at the public comment session that the proposed Dollar General was not, a harmonious use according to the town Code 108-116 A. (1), and that town officials had failed to properly examine the: "Harmonious relationship between the proposed uses and existing adjacent uses."

The key term here is "adjacent." Merriam Webster's Collegiate Dictionary, Tenth Edition, tells us "adjacent" means, "Not distant, being in close proximity"

In response to the public comment sessions' overwhelming condemnation of the town board's failure to enforce Code 108-116 A. (1), The Broadway Group, the applicant—not the town's planning board—hastily prepared its 4-29-21 report to shield the planning board members from the citizens' charge that Code Section 108-116 A. (1) was not being enforced.

Rather than prepare its own response to the public's rage expressed at the public comment sessions, the Town and Planning Board members eagerly latched onto the Broadway Group's twisted view of land use planning and development in the Colden Hamlet.

The planning board members never, before or after the public comment sessions, publicly addressed the requirements of Code 108-116 A. (1). Instead, they allowed the Broadway Group, acting not as an applicant, but as consultant to the planning board, to make the decisions for them.

Desperate to put to rest this harmonious relationship review requirement, here is how the planning board chairman, one day later, in an April 30, 2021 email, endorsed The Broadway Groups' April 29, 2021 report.

"The Broadway Group really addressed all the topics which I asked for in their letter and attachments, including a proper evaluation of the "harmonious use" matter which was already addressed by the planning board in our first meeting via our comparison of permitted uses in a commercial zone as well as the adjacent RRB zoning district.

The Broadway Group's analysis carries it to the next level, including a review of similar structures and uses. The planning board will review this also during our meeting since that came up more than expected at the recent public comment meetings."

And, on page 4 of the Final Planning Board Advisory Recommendation to the town board, dated May 12, 2021, is found another example of how eagerly the planning board members adopted The Broadway Group's report—without giving the public their critical review of the report; without any analysis of the report's accuracy, or whether it fairly addressed the citizens' complaints raised at the April 22, 2021 public comment sessions.

" Subsequent to the public comment session the applicant did a supplemental submission of site drawings…as well as a narrative document which detailed some responses to issues raised by the public in attendance at the two public comment sessions on 4.22.21. These documents were immediately made available to the Planning Board members who reviewed and considered them well prior to our May 6, 2021 Special Meeting."

The Broadway Group's report attempted—but failed—to show that the proposed Dollar General is a harmonious fit within the adjacent residential dwellings. Here are relevant passages from the Broadway Group's April 29, 2021 letter and report to Walt Kammer, Planning Board Chairman.

"The following review of section 108-116 (items A1-A4) provides a comprehensive examination of the criteria to be considered by the Planning Board recommendations.

"Section 108-116 Criteria for Planning Board Consideration

A. The Planning Board shall review the site plan and supporting data before making its recommendation to the Town Board and take into consideration the following: (1) Harmonious relationship between the proposed uses and existing adjacent uses. Response…

"Surrounding Uses. The Route 240 corridor is currently a mix of uses including commercial, residential and municipal. Residential uses are located at the North and South of the Project site. The adjacent and nearby built environment includes Colden Dental Care, Essentially Well Oiled, Colden Mill, Wellness Center, Colden Kitchen, Colden Country Inn, Colden Ski & Board Shop, Mayback's Small Engine Shop, Southtown's Tireman and Colden Market &Café…

"The Proposed Action will not have a significant impact on community character including existing and nearby land uses and character of adjacent and nearby commercial uses…

"Conclusion. The applicant respectfully submits that all criteria from Section 108-116 have been sufficiently considered. The Proposed Action is harmonious with adjacent uses…It is requested that the Planning Board make a favorable recommendation to the Town Board and that the Applicant be granted final site approval with a negative SEQR declaration [by the Town Board]."

Signed, Tara Mathias, Development Manager, The Broadway Group

*****

Ms. Mathias' argument is simple. It goes like this. Wearing her land use planner's hat, she classified the entire Route 240 through the Colden Hamlet—all the way from the Post Office in the north, to the Southtown's Tireman in the south— as a single, harmonious mixture of commercial and residential structures.

In her view, any newly proposed commercial structure—without regard to its location along Route 240, or its architectural consistency and harmonious fit with adjacent residential land uses—automatically forms an agreeable and harmonious relationship with adjacent properties.

The problem with Ms. Mathias' argument is also simple. It goes like this. The Colden Hamlet along Route 240—from the Post Office in the north to Southtown's Tireman in the south—is not a single, homogeneous mixed use zone as Ms. Mathias claims.

Instead, the Hamlet has, over the years, developed into two separate and distinct land use zones along Route 240: One residential zone to the north and the other, a mixed residential/commercial zone, to the south.

Take a look at Map 3. The proposed (now built) Dollar General store, located smack in the middle of an existing residential area, is obviously not a harmonious fit. And, it is also obviously not a part of the town's mixed commercial/residential zone located thousands of feet away, south of the Route 240/Boston-Colden/Heath Roads intersection.

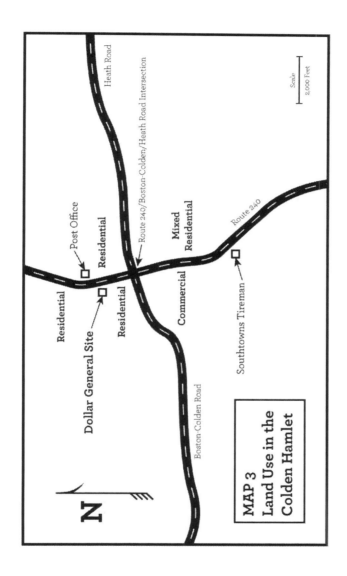

MAP 3
Land Use in the
Colden Hamlet

Not one of the businesses cited above by Ms. Mathias—Colden Dental Care, Essentially Well Oiled, Colden Mill, Wellness Center, Colden Kitchen, Colden Country Inn, Colden Ski & Board Shop, Mayback's Small Engine Shop, Southtown's Tireman and Colden Market &Café—is located in the residential zone north of the Route 240 intersection with Boston/Colden and Heath Roads.

The entire mixed commercial/residential zone is south of that intersection, thousands of feet from the Dollar General site and, certainly not as the town supervisor asserted in his Part 3 declaration, "…businesses in the immediate vicinity of the proposed [Dollar General] site."

It is not possible for the applicant or the planning board to make a convincing case that the proposed Dollar General store is a harmonious use, per Code 108-116 A. (1). Instead, a strong case can be made that the only location a Dollar General could be considered a harmonious use is in the existing, mixed use zone of the Hamlet, south of the Route 240/Boston-Colden/Heath Roads intersection.

Ms. Mathias failed to make a convincing case that the proposed Dollar General store was a harmonious use with its adjacent properties north of the Route 240/Boston-Colden/Heath Roads intersection. The question remains: Why did town and planning board members in the Town of Colden so eagerly adopt Ms. Mathias' faulty view of the Hamlet's land use pattern and her bogus application of the town's harmonious use law, Code 108-116 A. (1)?

Why did the town's planning board members—the town's planning "experts"—fail to protect and preserve the Hamlet's existing two-zone land development pattern?

Ms. Mathias' argument may have been faulty, but it fit with:

o The town and planning board's desperate attempt to redefine "harmonious relationship" at the June 3, 2021 town board workshop and to effectively eliminate Code 108-1116 A. (1) from their decision-making strategy; and,

o The Change-of-Use rule that conveniently removed the concerns of the residents living north of the Route 240/Boston-Colden/Heath Roads intersection, and most impacted by the proposed Dollar General, from the town's decision-making process.

o Planning boards in the Towns of Boston and Hamburg employed the assistance and expertise of certified land use planners. This was not the case in the Town of Colden where the planning board members acted more as rule-bound bureaucrats than capable land use planners.

CHAPTER 10. YOUR TURN

On Page 1, we set out to uncover the decision-making process used by each town to answer this question: Is the applicant's proposed location for building a Dollar General outlet consistent with the existing character of the neighboring community?

I have had my say. It is time for you—public administration & public policy students, small town administrators, land use planners and concerned citizens—drawing on the foregoing, three-town, comparative case study—to determine for yourself how well, or poorly, each town answered that question.

Take another look at the decision-making trail provided by the meeting minutes and the concerns voiced by citizens in their letters and emails.

What does this all add up to? Possible factors to consider in your assessment might include:

o Were planning board members in each town properly trained to do their job?

o How well did planning and town board members balance their—potentially conflicting—

responsibilities to consider the interests of the town's citizens and the interests of the developer?

o Did the involvement of professional land use planners in the Towns of Boston and Hamburg make a difference?

o Public officials in the Towns of Colden and Boston, operating under almost identical state and local zoning laws arrive at starkly different verdicts. How is this possible?

AFTERWORD

As is the often the case, after a study has been completed, relevant information not available while the study is underway, becomes available. In this case, the added information provides important insights into the thinking of Town of Colden officials during their Dollar General site plan review.

In reply to my question, "Why did the town not respond to citizen letters regarding the Dollar General proposal?" Mr. DePasquale wrote in his November 28, 2022 letter:

"The Town Board took all correspondence received into account…Please remember during a change of use public input is not required when the use is an allowed use in the zoned district which this case was. The Town Board went over and above the required process."

*****

In general, meeting minutes suggest Town of Colden Planning Board members did not adequately discuss and consider the impact of the proposed Dollar General on the adjacent residential properties. Mr. Walt Kammer, the board chairman, in his July 14, 2023 email, wrote:

"Per guidance from Town Attorney, the Chairman's personal attorney, and resources in Albany, the relevant factors…are NOT solely the immediate adjacent or adjoining parcels but rather the wider view for a reasonable and customary distance around the proposed action [the proposed Dollar General site.]"

APPENDIX A

Citizen Letters & Emails Sent to Town of Colden Officials

Regarding a Proposed Dollar General Store at
8680 State Road, Colden, NY

Name & Address	Impact of a Dollar General on Community Character
Ronald Roman February 18, 2021 email	To: Walter Kammer It has come to the attention of many Residents of Colden that a Dollar General is being proposed in our beautiful little town. Many if not all residents love the town of Colden for its quaint and beautiful charm.; A Dollar General right in the middle of our town not only doesn't belong with the image of our town but serves zero purpose other than to hurt the local economy and lower property values to the surrounding residents. Look at the Nextdoor app and see for yourself how many people are genuinely upset and angry over this proposed eyesore coming to our town.

Don Meissner on Burr Road February 18, 2021 email	To: Walter Kammer I am very much against putting a Dollar General in the Town of Colden. People live here because it is beautiful. The American people are feeling more and more that they are not being heard by many of our elected officials. I hope and pray that is not the case in Colden.
Gary & Judy Willert, 9073 Maltby Dr. Colden March 17, 2021	To: James DePasquale Dollar General is not an asset for our small town. There are Dollar Generals in Holland and E. Aurora. Colden does not need this dingy establishment.
Bob & June Pyne 8698 State Rd. Colden March 21, 2021	To: The Colden Town Board The lot line is 15 feet from our home…Who will compensate us for the loss of value of our home and property we have invested so much time, work and money in? Cars starting, doors slamming, truck deliveries…

Claire Nelligan Murry Hill Rd. Colden March 25, 2021	To: Town Board Members 　We want to keep our town attractive…such an unacceptable idea just to make money instead of beautifying our beautiful town. 　People can go to Springville, Orchard Park or Hamburg to get cheap items made in China.
An email from: tbrick April 1, 2021	To: James DePasquale Are you folks really all caving in to Dollar General?
"Concerned citizens" letter signed by 57 residents April 7, 2021	To: Town Board Members 　We write today as Town of Colden residents, voters and residents of property directly bordering where a Dollar General store is planned…we ask you to table this matter until the public can be given basic information as required by law.

Lara Hrycik 8728 Lower East Hill. Colden May 4, 2021	To: Walter Kammer & James DePasquale The adjacent properties are single family homes…I do not believe a retail store with cars projected to be in and out every 10-15 minutes, deliveries, etc., that this would be a harmonious use.
William & Barbara Baker, 8322 Creek End Rd., Colden May 5, 2021	To: Walter Kammer & James DePasquale Town Supervisor The planning board has not mentioned, regarding town code 108-116, how a 9,100 sq/ft building fits into that neighborhood to be flanked by single family homes built in the late19th and early 20th centuries. This is a failure of your fiduciary responsibility to preserve and promote the attractiveness of the town.
Thomas Baker May 5, 2021	To: Walter Kammer Regarding Town Code 108-116, harmonious use of the proposed site…there has not even been a mention of the Planning Board's perspective on how a 9100 sq/ft block building fits into that neighborhood…I ask kindly for you to make a recommendation to the Town Board that the Development site plan does not

	meet the requirements of Town Code 108-116 as the project is not in congruent use with adjoining properties and those properties in that neighborhood are all single residential in nature.

James Baker
 	
May 5, 2021
	To: Walter Kammer & James DePasquale
	
	   To this point there has not been a debate on the Planning Board's perspective on Town Code Section 108-116 A (1), on how a 9,100 sq/ft block building fits into that particular neighborhood and flanked by single-family homes built in the late 19th and early 20th century. This seems at minimum arbitrary and potentially capricious and is a failure of fiduciary responsibility on behalf of the citizenry and
	   The ZBA Chairman,
	Mr. Webster…admitted he may have made a mistake approving fewer parking slots. In general I feel the Town Board has appeared to be in a defensive position in the matter…and the tone and tenor of the relationship between the planning board, the town board and the applicant seems very comfortable and NOT reassuring as a citizen in opposition to the proposed Dollar General store.

Edward Kollatz May 6, 2021	To: Walter Kammer I urge you to act within the scope of the Town Codes you have sworn to dutifully execute. Most notably 108-116. Before seeing yourself as an authoritarian governing body, please see yourself as a neighbor and a community member first…put yourself in the citizens' shoes…make a recommendation to not grant the change of use citing Town Code 108-116 relative to harmonious use.
William & Barbara Baker, 8322 Creek End Rd, Colden May 10, 2021	To: James DePasquale This proposed project would not have a "harmonious relationship" to the surrounding properties as the Board is required to take into account.

Cynthia Lankenau 9002 Sunset Dr, Colden	To: Mr. DePasquale
	
	    The board is required to consider Section 108-116 of the town code. The proposed project would not have a harmonious relationship with existing adjacent uses—single family homes.
	    We have heard from various Town of Colden

May 11, 2021	officials that since the change of use is compliant with zoning requirements there is nothing they can do and they must approve this plan… [Editor's Note: Compliance with the town's zoning ordinance requires compliance with Section 108-116, since it too is part of the zoning ordinance.]
Linda Thomas, 8557 Finch Rd., Colden May 12, 2021	To: Supervisor DePasquale I support the issues raised in Peter Baker's May 10, 2021 letter to the town board, including that the proposed Dollar General would not have a harmonious relationship with the surrounding properties.
Protest Petition from neighbor-hood residents: the Bakers the Hudsons; Frank Giancola; Bob &	To: Town Board Members & Supervisor DePasquale To date, no one has even tried to explain why section 108-116a of the Town of Colden Code (the town's local law) is not even being considered in this change of use. We feel this is a failure of leadership. The very real concerns of the citizens are minimized while town officials use language in favor of the developer—'The developer has the

June Pyne; the Murray Family; and the Spagnola Family and Jessi Penfoid June 2, 2021	right' in support of the developer's proposal. 　　This language shows an unwillingness to consider Section 108-116 A of the town's zoning ordinance on behalf of us residents. 　　But I must say, I have written letters, made declarations and have been actively engaged in trying to delay for the purpose of clarity, and not one of you on the Board, including Mr. DePasquale, have even responded to my requests in any capacity...you have here a citizen who is very passionate about the matter and trying to be a voice of reason for others on the adjacent neighborhood. We feel let down that officials of this small town have decided to minimize us while the Broadway Group's representative has been actively involved in every meeting. 　　Somehow we are regarded as a nuisance because we are trying to protect what we have decided is our own self-determination before the Broadway Group arrived. 　　Signed, Peter Baker
Peter Baker, 8670 State Rd.; Debi Baker, 8670 State Rd.;	To: James Depasquale, Town Supervisor 　　Throughout this process, the developer has been granted extensive access to the Town Board and other town officials, while local citizens, residents and taxpayer have been

Bob & June Pyne, 8698 State Rd.; Butch & Bernie Hudson, 8693 State Rd.; and Frank Giancola, 8693 state Rd. Colden
 	
June 7, 2021
	permitted to speak once.
	    The Board is required to take into account the harmonious relationship between the proposed uses and existing adjacent uses—single family homes.
	    We have heard comments from various Town of Colden officials over the past few months that since this change-of-use is compliant with zoning requirements, there is nothing they can do, and must approve this plan.
	    At the June 3, 2021 town board workshop it was said that any use permitted by the zoning code is inherently harmonious. Per our attorney, this statement has no legal basis.
	    As concerned citizens and adjacent neighbors to the proposed Dollar General site, we feel extremely let down by our town leaders and their failure to react to this proposal in the interest of the Town of Colden citizens.
	    Still, to this date, none of you have responded to letters and emails requesting to be put on the agenda at meetings where these matters were discussed…
	    And to hear our town leaders repeatedly say things like 'We don't have to have public hearings for a change of use' is cowardly, and a gross negligence of your official duties to protect the interests of the town and the citizens therein.
	    Signed, Peter Baker

Ronald Hensel, 9208 Center Rd, Colden July 10, 2021	To: Members of the Town Board Section 108-116 A, (1) of the town code is not being considered. The developer only has the right to apply for change of use, but no guarantee that they will get the change. The Dollar General will create a visual malignancy both day and night. It is a travesty to the architectural flavor of the town and neighborhood.
Joseph Murray, 8742 State Road, Colden No date	To: Members of the Town Board This project will significantly affect our beautiful residential neighborhood, our quality of life. It is not something the neighborhood needs. We have plenty of stores close by that can satisfy anything that store can provide.

One Dollar General Too Far

About the Author

Long ago, working as an economic development planner at the Appalachian Regional Commission, I first became acquainted with the nature of public administration in small towns from Ohio to Mississippi.

Then, the 1957 book, *Grass Roots: Rural Democracy in America*, by Syracuse University professor, Roscoe C. Martin—a critical account of the unique public management problems historically rooted in small, rural towns—rounded-out my interest in this neglected corner of public administration.

Prior studies include: *To Frack or Not to Frack: How a Small New York Town's Decision-Making Process Came-up Short*, (2018), and *America, Democracy and YOU: Where Have all the Citizens Gone?* (2015). Both are also available from Amazon.

For decades a Washington-based writer specializing in public policy/public management issues, I now live in the Buffalo, New York area with my wife, PJ, two dogs, Max and Nella, and Felix the cat.

Made in the USA
Middletown, DE
23 October 2023

41129872R00088